A MILLION SHADOWS AT NOON

Lenard D. Moore
with
Preface by Ce Rosenow
and
Introduction by Jerry W. Ward, Jr.
and
Afterword by E. Ethelbert Miller

A Million Shadows at Noon

© 1996, 2004, 2006, and 2023 by Lenard D. Moore

Preface Copyright © 2023 by Ce Rosenow

Introduction Copyright © 1996, 2004, 2006, and 2023 by Jerry W. Ward, Jr.

Afterword Copyright © 1996, 2004, 2006, and 2023 by E. Ethelbert Miller

All Rights Reserved

First Printing

ISBN 978-1-7350257-6-6

CUTTLEFISH
BOOKS

ACKNOWLEDGEMENTS

Grateful appreciation is offered to the editors and publishers of *Drumvoices Review* and *Papyrus* in which some of these poems have previously appeared.

The poems "gathering place," "autumn dawn," "the cadenced footsteps," "sun plaza:" "the speaker's hand," "on the stage," "on the marble bench," "lingering wind," "darkening day" and "night after the march" were also published in the collaborative chapbook *Gathering At The Crossroads* with photographs by Eugene B. Redmond (Red Moon Press, 2003).

AUTHOR'S NOTE

In this book, I aim to present deeper insights into the unfolding of The Million Man March. I purposely repeat autumn and fall throughout this book to show a stark contrast between autumn and the million Black men. Autumn is when leaves change from green to red, yellow, and gold. This season is as beautiful as the faces of my people—the black/brown/yellow faces engaged at The March. Just like autumn, we, as a people, are changing. We come together peacefully to save our communities, our families, ourselves. In spite of negative media coverage, the Black man is human. I hope that this long poem/sequence engages my readers to the point of understanding the Black man's struggle. I used a "Million Men" repeatedly in this book to evoke the magnitude of so many Black men coming together, to deepen the meaning of it all, and to resonate like a blues song heard for the first time. Perhaps this poem/sequence causes one to reconsider the plight of the darker brother. Here are the images and the sounds of The Million Man March.

Lenard D. Moore
Raleigh, North Carolina, USA
January 28, 1996

PREFACE

In *A Million Shadows at Noon*, Lenard D. Moore constructs an extended haiku sequence about the Million Man March that took place in Washington, D. C. on October 16, 1995. Moore documents many singular moments from the march and arranges them in chronological order to place readers at the event and to create a communal narrative.

Haiku may seem an unusual choice for crafting a narrative let alone for sharing a group's experience because haiku are momentary in nature and often present an individual's reality. Haiku sequences, however, provide the opportunity for a narrative approach to a topic because they present several haiku, usually under a unifying title, and connect them by a theme or subject. Moore is a gifted writer of haiku sequences, including extended haiku sequences as seen in his book, *Desert Storm*. In *Desert Storm* and in *A Million Shadows at Noon*, he skillfully focuses on key moments while linking those moments together over time.

Moore uses several haiku techniques in varying combinations to convey the specific moments: juxtaposed images, an internal comparison or relationship between those images, a pivot or shift in the middle of the poem resulting in a surprising moment of awareness at the poem's conclusion, and a *kigo* or seasonal reference. Rather than painting the experiences of African American men with broad strokes, Moore focuses on vivid, momentary instances that resonate with readers and remain in their memories. At the same time, he uses the extended sequence form to draw together single moments from multiple perspectives. The collection doesn't provide the story of one man but of many such that it conveys the experience of the group. The sequence is also comprised of moments that depict the beginning, middle, and end of the march, thereby constructing a complete narrative.

    Throughout the book, Moore documents aspects of the march that emphasize his statement in the Author's Note that "the Black man is human" and contribute to the overall sense of unity among the participants. He depicts moments of collective action, such as marching, praying, and chanting, and he also emphasizes the bond of brotherhood shared by men. For example, many of these poems focus on the vast number of men participating in the march and the bond that they share. These haiku support Moore's belief that "the magnitude of so many Black men coming together . . . might lead one to reconsider the plight of the darker brother."

> autumn plaza
> a million shadows at noon
> strong men marching
>
> three weeks into fall—
> one million brothers stand tall
> oaks sway mutely

The "autumn plaza" title haiku of the book combines the images of the men marching and the shadows they cast. By using "a million" in reference to the shadows, Moore creates an internal comparison between the number of shadows and the number of men. The "million shadows" suggest the impact of so many men marching together, casting their shadows across the public and politicized space of the plaza and further emphasizing physical presence and strength. Marching itself has historical significance not only in terms of protests in general but, more specifically for African American culture, the marches of the Civil Rights Movement. Finally, marching requires that the men move in unison, as a single body comprised of a million individual bodies.

While some poems represent the sense of brotherhood among the men, others address individual family units. These poems speak not only to the humanity of the participants but also to unity sustained on a smaller scale. Moore dedicates both collections to "Jerome Moore, Ron Moore, Rodney Moore, Marvin Moore (my brothers) and especially for Angela Moore and Wanda Moore Mulvaney (my sisters)," suggesting his investment in the importance of the march for individual families including his own. The following haiku exemplifies unity on a smaller scale by focusing on the relationship between father and son:

>   autumn dawn—
>   a father briefing his son
>   in the parking lot

A Million Shadows at Noon concludes with the following poem, drawing together the multiple emphases on Moore's individual haiku moments and larger narratives about the march participants and African American men:

> night after the march
> reading the million-man pledge
> to my pregnant wife

Just as the sequence is prefaced by a dedication to Moore's siblings, it concludes with an image of Moore's own family. Like the haiku about the father and son in the parking lot, this poem reveals that the impact of the march will last into the future. Moore reads the pledge to his pregnant wife, and the reader understands that his commitment to the pledge will have an impact not only on his wife but on his future child. It is a haiku moment specifically experienced by Moore, but it also resonates with the other moments in the sequence. Rather than simply refer to the pledge, Moore describes it as "the million-man pledge," emphasizing the large number of men who committed to follow it. Moore maps his individual story onto their stories, and the combination creates a larger communal narrative for African American men in general. Through this final haiku and those that precede it, Moore presents single, transitory moments to create a communal narrative about the strength, commitment, and humanity of African American men.

Ce Rosenow
author, *Lenard D. Moore and African American Haiku: Merging Traditions*
Senior Editor, *Juxtapositions: Research and Scholarship in Haiku*

THE OCULAR VOICE

Lenard D. Moore's *A Million Shadows At Noon* is a poetic memoir of a day of atonement, that fateful gathering in Washington, D.C. on October 16, 1995 where a million plus men willed to absent themselves from the banality of human evil. It was a special moment in the history of African American emotions, and it resists having its symbolism resymbolized. The March, or our memory of the ritual, does not resist serving as the ground for creation. As one of the leading haiku poets in the United States, Moore understands how deceptively simple forms can be used to make complexity accessible. His earlier book, *Desert Storm: A Brief History* (1993), demonstrates how an Oriental form can enable a poet to avoid some of the limitations of Occidental narrative poetry. We do not need yet another narrative about October 16, 1995. We do welcome a poem that enables us to recollect our powerful emotional responses to that day and to consider how dim or vivid are our memories now.

However much this poem reminds us of Moore's earlier work, it does represent a departure. Here the poet has conceptualized his poem as a space for the ocular voice, the voice that is intimately linked with the photographic and with the hearer's use of words as tools for visualizing. Each segment (or caption as it were) demands our supplying a relevant image from our visual archive—depth, color, magnitude, texture, shape, illumination. Such a demand is implicit in the philosophical underpinning of haiku. But the haiku segments in *A Million Shadows At Noon* are not independent instances. Each is a stage in a movement from dawn to dusk to the newly promised dawn. As we experience the full movement, we begin to sense how radical, successful, and empowering the poem is. Like Sterling A. Brown's "Strong Men," this poem is a well crafted example of how the poet induces readers to engage in aesthetic/political activity.

After we have photomemoried *A Million Shadows At Noon*, we discover the anticipated future is brought to personal closure. The dominance of the optical is displaced by sound, the invisible eye being transformed into the speaking subject. The silent witness is embodied fully as

> night after the march
> reading the million-man pledge
> to my pregnant wife

the poet/photographer elicits the absent vows

I will	strive	to love, to improve, to build
	will never	raise my hand/abuse my wife/ engage in abuse of children/ use the "B" word
	will not	poison my body
	will	support, do all this

At the final center of remembering is man speaking to woman who contains and nurtures the promised future, the child as continuity, biological verity, and love!

In the end of *A Million Shadows At Noon* is the initial moment Lenard D. Moore and his readers share.

Jerry W. Ward, Jr.
Moss Chair of Excellence in English
University of Memphis
March 17, 1996

A MILLION SHADOWS AT NOON

driving off to march...
young men wearing wool hats
black with autumn

gathering place—
bus after bus idling
as the sun comes up

slow sunrise—
where the fallen leaves end
the man's wheelchair gleams

the charred bus
moves through falling leaves—
the men chatter

autumn dawn—
a father briefing his son
in the parking lot

buses parked:
   the million black men gather...
    falling October leaves

lane to the park—
closing the car door
a gust of autumn

frostless morning
still breath clouds rise
where stern men meet

fall morning sunlight
old man puts million-man pledge
in his suit pocket

autumn deepens—
dreadlocked brothers on the street
ready to march

the opening march...
the crown of his shaved head
blotched with fall sun

two-lane street—
one by one the men keep coming
into fall light

sun wind
left/right rhythm of black boys
steps higher

the cadenced footsteps
of one million black men—
a warm fall day

autumn plaza
a million shadows at noon
strong men marching

still marching
sun lengthens on the asphalt street
a million black men

sun plaza:
one million shadows darken
foot by foot

march route—
changing the camera's film
beneath unmoving clouds

wind stirs his black beard
the photographer snaps shots
of one million men

minister's voice rises
over one million black men
faint gold of trees

autumn light—
the woman poet reading
to the plaza crowd

the speaker's hand
bends the microphone down
deepening autumn

on the stage
a line of brothers lock arms
autumn sunshine

no fall sounds—
just the rich black song
of a million men

million-man march—
each one sings the same tune
autumn day

praying
in the fall wind,
one million men

blowing with the wind
red leaves on a stand of trees
the men keep praying

three weeks into fall—
one million brothers stand tall
oaks sway mutely

October 16th—
a young boy raises his fist
near the marble statue

on the statue's base
million-man march poster curls
warm October sun

on the marble bench
a zipped-up windbreaker
autumn wind

warm wind of fall—
black tints of wavering flags
in the million march

autumn day—
in the moving capital light
the million men

October gust—
middle-aged man wipes dust
off his eyeglasses

wind plaza:
a yellow leaf blowing
the way of the men

a day on Washington—
booming beneath the fall sky
one million chants

lingering wind
the chant of black men goes on
this autumn day

bright autumn sky—
　the darker faces
　　of a million marching men

million-man march in fall
sunblanched footsteps marking time
on the concrete mall

low wind...
man after man highstepping
into evening

marching on
   the countless men this fall day
backs to the sun

autumn—
rap song on the red boombox
thumping

autumn evening
one by one the buses leave
the reserved parking lot

buses winding home—
the chants of one million men
still resonate

last glimmer
of the autumn sun...
tap of blind man's cane

darkening sky
a row of folding chairs
left in the plaza

twilight plaza
the ghosts of ancestors
still marching

where black men once marched
through autumn daylight
the street sweeper sweeps

night after the march
reading the million-man pledge
to my pregnant wife

BODIES AND SOULS

As I write this Afterword to Lenard D. Moore's *A Million Shadows At Noon*, there is still considerable discussion of the Million Man March and Louis Farrakhan taking place within the African American community and in the general media. This is of no surprise when we think of the historical importance of the March held on October 16, 1995 in Washington, D.C. What took place on that day was a tremendous outpouring of love and solidarity expressed between African American men of all ages. The event rejected the negative images too often associated with black masculinity. When the concept of brotherhood is discussed in the future, I am certain we will refer to the Million Man March. Remembering the March is something writers and photographers have already done. There are several books which have been published that provide pictures, speeches, commentary and analysis of the march. *A Million Shadows At Noon* therefore, must be seen in the context of documentation and poetry.

Lenard D. Moore has written a long poem consisting of fifty parts. He describes the day of the Million Man March from morning until evening. His use of the long poem places him within the African American literary tradition upheld by Melvin Tolson and Langston Hughes. Hughes 1951, *Montage of A Dream Deferred* was crafted in such a way that bebop rhythms helped to move the poem along at a fast pace, as Hughes captured the many sounds and voices of the Harlem community. In *A Million Shadows At Noon*, each section of Moore's poem is similar to a photograph. Instead of a montage, Moore presents us with a collage of images. Each section of the poem encourages the reader to reflect on a moment in time. A key aspect of the March was that the spiritual-51-message of the march had been felt, which could not be captured primarily by visual images. The march was a "soulful" event which could only be measured by the things not seen. It is here where poetry begins, the point where the heart understands love and where the human spirit depends on faith. As poets how do we sing this song of celebration?

My interpretation of *A Million Shadows At Noon* is that it is a book of "ritual" by an African American male poet. It is as ambitious as the march itself. The poetry invites us to board a bus and travel to the march. What unfolds is Moore's long poetic sequence and the observation of a political event against the background of seasonal change; the season is autumn not spring. One ponders if this is the status of the political struggle of African American. Moore's observation in one section of *A Million Shadows At Noon* reflect the following:

> fall morning sunlight
> old man puts million-man pledge
> in his suit pocket

Has the old man been a witness to these types of gatherings? Has he heard the speeches and pledges before? How are we to interpret the line "fall morning sunlight" without thinking about the twilight of our struggle? Is the image one of light at the end of the tunnel? Still, the old man's placing of the pledge in his suit pocket is representative of our quiet dignity...and somehow we continue to survive.

At times it is difficult to determine if Moore is simply observing the march, or if his poem is intended to call us back together. The last section of the poem reminds us that this book is one man's description of what took place on October 16, 1995. However, just as many have concluded that the Million Man March was bigger than Louis Farrakhan, so it is with *A Million Shadows At Noon*. This long poem composed by Lenard D. Moore is a tribute to the many faces and voices who came to Washington, D.C. for this historical event. African American men are celebrated in fifty sections; and reflect new images of ourselves.

Lenard D. Moore has given us more than a pledge; he has given us the gift of Poetry. African American men should march for nothing less.

E. Ethelbert Miller
Jessie Ball duPont Visiting Scholar
Emory & Henry College
March 17, 1996

ABOUT THE AUTHOR

Lenard D. Moore, a native of Jacksonville, North Carolina, where he attended Onslow County Public Schools and graduated from White Oak High School, is a poet, essayist, playwright, fiction writer, literary consultant, editor, critic, public speaker, workshop conductor, teacher, son, husband, and father. His poems, reviews, and essays have appeared in more than 350 magazines, newspapers, and anthologies in more than a dozen countries. His works have been published in *The Garden Thrives* (HarperCollins, 1996), *Soulfires* (Penguin USA, 1996), *In Search Of Color Everywhere* (Stewart, Tabori, & Chang, 1994), *I Hear A Symphony* (Anchor Books, 1994), *The Haiku Anthology* (Norton, 1999), and others. He is the author of *Desert Storm: A Brief History* (Los Hombres Press, 1993), *Forever Home* (St. Andrews College Press, 1992), and *The Open Eye* (The North Carolina Haiku Society Press, 1985). Mr. Moore is the recipient of the Haiku Museum of Tokyo Award (2003, 1994 and 1983), and numerous other awards. He has read his poetry on numerous TV shows, radio programs ("Voice of America"), at colleges and universities, conferences, festivals (National Black Arts Festival, 2002, 2000, 1998, 1996, 1992), cultural centers (Walt Whitman Cultural Arts Festival, 1995), art galleries, schools, churches, and libraries (The Library of Congress, 1986). He reviews books for a number of publications. He has taught at Enloe High School; NC A & T State University; NC State University; . In 1987, Moore began working in the Poet-in-the-Schools, conducting writing workshops in classrooms throughout Wake County. He is presently working on a novel, a full-length play, three collections of poetry, and short stories. He lives in Raleigh where he taught English, world literature, and humanities at Shaw University. He is past two-term president of the Haiku Society of America. He also is past Honorary Curator of the American Haiku Archives at the California State Library in Sacramento.

www.ingramcontent.com/pod-product-compliance
Lightning Source LLC
Chambersburg PA
CBHW061740070526
44585CB00024B/2755